HOOTIE
JOINS IN

By Marcie Heller Aboff
Illustrated by Joy Allen

Credits

Illustrations: Joy Allen

Computer colorizations by Lucie Maragni

Cover and book design by Lisa Ann Arcuri

ISBN 0-7652-1365-6

Printed in the United States of America
8 9 10 11 12 VON4 13 12 11 10

Modern Curriculum Press

Pearson Learning Group

1-800-321-3106
www.pearsonlearning.com

Contents

To my mother and father
MHA

To my daughter Beverly,
"My new songbird."
JA

Chapter 1
Moving

Hootie could not sleep. He had dark circles under his big round eyes. All day long, cars and trucks honked and beeped. The noise was keeping Hootie awake.

"I have to do something," Hootie said. "What can I do?"

Hootie thought and thought. Then he had an idea. "I'll move to a new tree. I'll find one that is far away from all the cars and trucks," Hootie said.

Hootie began to pack his bags. The sun was setting behind the tall city buildings when he finished.

"Good-bye, old tree," he said. "I'm moving to a place where it is quiet."

Hootie flew off. He flew over many trees in a big park. Some trees were tall, but their branches were very thin. Some trees had thick branches, but those trees were very short. Then he saw a tall tree that was just right.

Hootie found a branch he liked. He worked all night setting up his bed.

At last, Hootie was ready to go to sleep. The early morning sun was just reaching Hootie's branch. Hootie closed his eyes. He began to fall asleep.

Suddenly, Hootie's eyes popped
open. He was so surprised, he nearly
fell out of his tree. "What was that
noise?" he asked.

Chapter 2
New Neighbors

Hootie stood up on his branch. He tried to see where the noise was coming from. "What's going on?" he cried.

A little brown bird looked down from a branch above Hootie. "Who are you?" the little brown bird asked Hootie.

"I'm Hootie. I'm trying to sleep, but I can't sleep. There is too much noise," said Hootie.

"But it is morning," said the bird. "It's time for birds to wake up."

"Not me," Hootie said. "Owls sleep during the day. Who are you?"

The little brown bird stood as tall as he could. "My name is Singer. I am a song sparrow. I love to sing songs."

"What's going on here?" asked a gray bird.

"This owl does not want us to sing in the daytime," said Singer. "He wants to sleep all day."

"Who are you?" asked Hootie.

"My name is Kitty," the gray bird said. "I am a catbird. I make all kinds of sounds. I can even sing 'meow' like a cat."

More birds poked their heads out
from behind the branches. They all
looked at Hootie. Singer said, "All the
birds in this tree sing. We are the Oak
Tree Songbirds."

Hootie looked angry. "Well, I need
to sleep!" he cried.

13

Singer pointed to a tree across the
park. "Why don't you sleep in that
tree?" he asked Hootie.

"It's too small," said Hootie.

Kitty pointed to another tree. "Why
don't you sleep in that tree?" she asked.

"No. It's too close to the cars," said
Hootie. "I want to sleep here."

The birds had a problem.

Chapter 3
Songbirds Must Sing

Kitty and Singer called all the Oak Tree Songbirds to a meeting. Singer spoke first. "We have lived together in this tree for a long time. We all love to sing, but what should we do about Hootie?"

"We were here first," said Kitty.
"Hootie should move."

"Hootie doesn't want to move," said
Singer.

All the birds thought for a long time.

Then a tiny bird with a short tail
chirped up. It was Rose. Rose was a
smart wren.

16

"Let's ask Hootie to sing with us," said Rose. "He can sing with us during the day and sleep all night."

"No," said Singer. "Hootie is an owl. Owls sleep all day and stay up all night."

"Let's ask him anyway," said Rose. So all the birds flew to find Hootie.

The birds found Hootie asleep in his
bed. "Wake up, wake up!" cried Kitty.

Hootie sat up. "What do you want
now?" he asked.

"Will you sing with the Oak Tree
Songbirds?" asked Singer.

Chapter 4
A Plan

Hootie did not know why the birds were asking him to sing. "I am not a songbird. I am an owl," he told the birds.

"We want you to sing with us," said Singer. "Maybe you could try staying awake during the day."

"What?" cried Hootie. "I have to sleep all day so I can hunt for food at night. I might sing with you, but not during the day."

The birds still had a problem. They were ready to give up and fly away.

Then Rose chirped up again. "We could sing early in the morning before Hootie goes to sleep. All the other birds would just be waking up."

"We could also sing in the evening before the songbirds go to sleep. Hootie would just be waking up," Singer added.

"Yes!" said the birds. Hootie nodded. The birds flew off to let Hootie sleep.

Chapter 5
Hootie Sings

That evening, just as the sun was beginning to set, Hootie heard the birds. He crawled out of bed to join them. Kitty was singing a tune.

"I am a catbird, shiny and gray.
I love to sing all through the day."
Then all the songbirds sang, "Woo, woo
. . . woo, woo."
Singer asked Hootie, "Will you sing
the last line with us?"

Singer began to sing.

"I am a sparrow with a voice so fine.
I love to sing, I really shine."

All the birds sang, "Woo, woo . . .
woo, woo."

Hootie sang, too.

"Wait!" said Kitty. She glared at Hootie. "You're not singing the right word. It's 'Woo, woo . . . woo, woo.' You're singing 'Hoo, hoo . . . hoo, hoo.'"

Hootie tried and tried, but he could not sing "woo, woo."

"Owls sing 'hoo, hoo,'" said Hootie.

All the birds shook their heads. It
seemed they had another problem.

Then Hootie started to smile. He had
an idea. Hootie told the others, "Let's
try again tomorrow. I think we'll be
better then."

Chapter 6
The Best Song Ever

The next morning, just as the sun was rising, the birds began to sing. Hootie joined them.

Hootie smiled as he sat among the songbirds. The songbirds did not smile.

Kitty flew to the front of the group.
She opened her wings wide.

Suddenly, Hootie started to sing. He
sang to Kitty, "Hoo, hoo. Who are you?"

Then Kitty sang.

"I am a catbird, shiny and gray.
I love to sing all through the day."

"That sounds great!" said Kitty.

Then Singer flew to the front of the group. Hootie sang to him, "Hoo, hoo. Who are you?"

Then Singer sang.

"I am a sparrow with a voice so fine. I love to sing, I really shine."

Hootie sang, "Hoo, hoo. Who are you?" to each songbird.

Only Hootie had not sung alone.
Then, all the birds sang to him, "Hoo,
hoo. Who are you?"

Hootie flew to the front and sang,
"I am an owl, spotted and brown.
My home is the best in all the town."

All the other birds clapped their wings and cheered. Then the birds looked around the tree. Lots of other birds were clapping their wings, too. They had flocked to the oak tree to hear the new song.

"Thanks, Hootie," said Kitty. "Our tree has the best singers in the park, and now only our tree has a singing owl."

31

Glossary

chirped [churpt] made a short, high sound

flocked [flahkt] traveled with a group

glared [glaird] stared angrily

poked [pohkt] pushed

shiny [SHYE nee] glowing, not dull

songbirds [SAWNG burdz] birds who sound as if they are singing

suddenly [SUD dun lee] quickly, by surprise

tune [toon] a song